INVESTIGATIONS IN RELIGION

The Life of Jesus

DAVID STENT

Basil Blackwell

Contents

Who Was Jesus?	3
What Did Jesus Look Like?	4
Did Jesus Exist?	6
The Record of Jesus' Life	8
Who Copied?	10
The Jesus of the Gospels	12
Where Jesus Lived	14
An Occupied Country	16
Jesus and the Synagogue	18
Pharisees and Sadducees	20
John the Baptist	22
The Essenes	24
Temptation	26
The Disciples	28
Miraculous Happenings	30
Jesus the Teacher	32
A New Religion?	34
One Week in a Short Life	36
The Last Night	38
Was Jesus a Criminal?	40
How Jesus Died	42
The Turin Shroud	44
What Happened on Easter Day?	46

First published 1986
Reprinted 1986, 1988

Published by
Basil Blackwell Ltd
108 Cowley Road
Oxford OX4 1JF

ISBN 0 631 90280 5

Printed in Hong Kong by Wing King Tong Co. Ltd.

All quotations from the Bible are from the Good News Bible, © American Bible Society 1966, 1971, 1976, published by the Bible Societies and Collins, and are used by permission.

Acknowledgements

The author and publishers would like to thank the following for permission to reproduce photographs:

Archaeological Museum of Istanbul 20A; The British Library 3A, 3B, 12A(4); The British Society for the Turin Shroud 44A, 44B, 44C; The Bible Society 22C, 24A, 42B; Camerapix/Hutchinson 30B; Peter Clayton 16D; Sonia Halliday Photographs 4B, 4D, 14C, 14D, 18A, 22B, 26C, 30A, 32B, 48B; BBC Hulton Picture Library 4A, 4C, 4E, 4F, 6D, 26A, 36B, 36F, 38C; Israeli Department of Antiquities and Museums 24B, 24C; Israel Exploration Journal 42D; Israeli Government Press Office 18C; Mandel Archives 22D; the Mansell Collection 16B, 22A, 28A, 30C, 32C, 42C; Middle East Photographic Archive 24A; Rylands Library 8B; Salesian Congregation 42A; York Minster 10D.

Cover: *The Calling of the Apostles Peter and Andrew*; DUCCIO di Buoninsegna; National Gallery of Art, Washington; Samuel H. Kress Collection.

Who Was Jesus?

Jesus has had a huge effect on millions of people's lives. He plays a part in your life every year – **A** and **B** are pictures of events in the life of Jesus which are marked by holidays in Christian countries. Do you know which ones?

It might seem surprising for someone so important but there is a lot we do not know about Jesus. For example, we do not know the exact year he was born or when he died. Historians think he must have been born in about 5 BC and that he probably died in about AD 30, but no one is certain.

Even though there is much that we do not know, there have been many claims made about Jesus. If you asked a group of people 'Who was Jesus?' you would get a lot of different answers. Some possible replies are –

- He lived nearly 2000 years ago in the country called Israel today
- He was crucified by the Romans
- He rose from the dead
- He was the Son of God
- He was a good man who healed the sick
- He started the Christian religion
- He is still alive today

Which of these statements do you think is correct? Perhaps you are not sure because some of them are very unusual things to say about someone. What is the evidence to support these claims?

In this book we are going to look at the evidence about Jesus and the world in which he lived to try and get a clear picture of who he was and see how he made such a big impression on those who met him.

What Did Jesus Look Like?

What do you think Jesus looked like? If the six people in pictures **A–F** were lined up in an identity parade, which one would you say was Jesus?

Did Jesus have a beard? Black hair or fair hair? Was there a halo round his head? Did he wear a crown? Did he look special or different from other people?

A–F are all pictures of Jesus. **A** is a painting from Rome, 16th century. **B** is a mosaic from Greece, 12th century. **C** is a painting from the tombs of the early Christians in Rome. It was probably painted in the 3rd century. **D** is from China, 19th century. **E** is from France, 17th century. **F** is from England, 19th century.

Each of these pictures shows Jesus in a different way. Were the artists trying to show what Jesus really looked like, or what he was like as a person, or what they thought he was like?

Today we can find out what someone looks like from photographs. But there are no photographs of Jesus – there were no cameras when he was alive nearly 2000 years ago. Though there are thousands of paintings of Jesus, like the ones **A–F**, not one was painted in his lifetime. No one knows what Jesus really looked like. We do not even have a description of what he looked like by anyone who knew him.

🌿 **Things to do** 🌿

1 Match one of the descriptions of Jesus, a–f, with each of the pictures **A–F**.
a) ordinary looking b) young c) angry
d) unhappy e) stern f) wise
Explain why you made your choices.

2 Why do you think Jesus is often shown with a beard when we do not know that he had one?

3 a) Which of the pictures **A–F** show Jesus with a halo? What is a halo?
b) Why do you think some artists gave Jesus a halo?

4 Do you think it matters whether we know what Jesus looked like? Explain the reasons for your answer.

Did Jesus Exist?

Most of what we know about Jesus was written by his followers, the early Christians. They wrote about Jesus to convince other people that he was special and had risen from the dead. Some people doubt what they tell us. Some people have wondered whether Jesus ever existed at all. Was the whole story made up?

There is some evidence about Jesus which was not written by the early Christians.

A was written by a Roman historian, called Tacitus, in about AD 115. Tacitus is explaining how the Roman Emperor Nero punished the Christians in Rome for the fire which destroyed much of that city in AD 64.

(A) *Nero blamed and tortured a group of people hated for their evil practices – a group popularly known as Christians. Christ (Jesus), from whom the group took their name, was put to death by Pontius Pilate, one of our governors, during the reign of the Emperor Tiberius. The deadly superstition, stopped for a while, broke out not only in Judaea, the first source of the evil, but also in Rome.*

Tacitus does not tell us much about Jesus. Josephus, another historian, writing in about AD 93, says more. Read **B**.

(B) *There was a wise man, Jesus the son of Joseph. Many people thought he was a wonder worker. He taught people who wanted to learn the truth and he won over many Judaeans and many foreigners. Those who followed him thought he was God's chosen leader.*

There is very little other evidence about Jesus from people who were not Christians. Is this surprising? If Jesus was as important as Christians claim, why was he not better known? **C** gives some reasons why non-Christian evidence about Jesus is so rare.

(C) 1 Jesus lived in an unimportant part of the world. Judaea was a small part of the Roman Empire. When Tacitus was writing, the Empire was large and powerful. He only mentions Jesus because of the Christians in Rome.
2 Jesus was born into an ordinary family. He was not a rich or powerful ruler.
3 There was no television and there were no newspapers 2000 years ago. News travelled slowly by word of mouth.
4 In Jesus' time there were many different religions practised in his part of the world. Josephus mentions other religious teachers like Jesus.

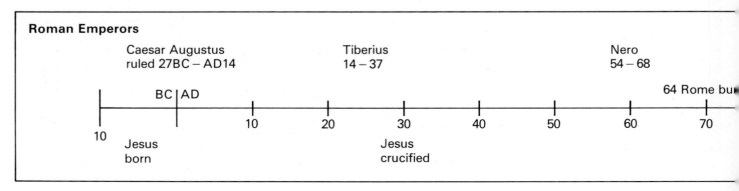

Roman Emperors

Caesar Augustus ruled 27BC – AD14

Tiberius 14 – 37

Nero 54 – 68

BC | AD

64 Rome bu[rnt]

10   20   30   40   50   60   70

10

Jesus born

Jesus crucified

D

Tacitus explains how Nero punished the Christians for the fire in Rome.

Insults of every sort were added to their deaths. Covered with the skins of animals, they were torn apart by dogs and killed. Some were fixed to crosses or burned to light up the night. Nero mingled with the people dressed like a charioteer.

E Time chart

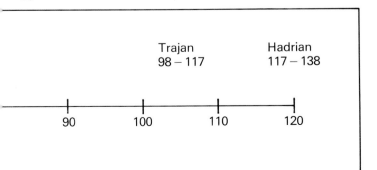

	Trajan 98 – 117	Hadrian 117 – 138
90	100 110	120

⊰⊱ **Things to do** ⊱⊰

1 a) What does Tacitus tell us about Jesus? Do you think he was sympathetic to Christianity? Why? b) What does Josephus tell us about Jesus? Do you think Josephus was sympathetic to Christianity? Why?

2 What is happening in the picture **D**? Imagine you were an onlooker. Describe the scene.

3 **E** is a time chart. Copy it out and put in the dates Josephus and Tacitus wrote their histories.

4 Do you think Tacitus and Josephus provide convincing evidence that Jesus existed? Give reasons for your answer.

The Record of Jesus' Life

Almost everything we know about Jesus is contained in four books called gospels. The word *gospel* means 'good news'. It was first used to describe the message of Jesus. Later it became the name for the books which contained the story of his life and teaching.

Who wrote the gospels? None of the four books tells us the name of its author or when it was written. Early Christian evidence says that Matthew, Mark, Luke and John wrote them and we still call the gospels by these names today. But modern experts think it is very doubtful whether Matthew, Mark, Luke and John really did write the gospels named after them.

Look carefully at **A** to see the difference between what Irenaeus said about the gospel writers in AD 175 and what historians think today.

We do not know exactly when the gospels were written because the original books have not survived, (see **B**). The evidence suggests that they were written between 30 and 70 years after Jesus was killed. Jesus had a great effect on his followers so why did they not write about him sooner?

1 At the time Jesus lived, books were less common than they are today. It was hard to produce a book then because there was no

(A)

Matthew's Gospel – written about AD 80, for Christians at Antioch, by a Jew who had become a Christian.
Irenaeus' view, that it was written by one of Jesus' disciples, Matthew, is unlikely. The writer does not show that he knew Jesus personally. A disciple of Jesus would show a closer personal knowledge of him.

Mark's Gospel – written AD 60–70, may have been written by someone living in Rome.
It is possible that the author was John Mark of Jerusalem, a companion of Paul on one of his missionary journeys. He may also have been a friend of Peter. Mark may have met Jesus but he would have been very young at the time Jesus was killed.

In about AD 175 a Christian called Irenaeus wrote –
Matthew published a written gospel for the Jews in their own language while Peter and Paul were preaching the gospel in Rome. After they died, Mark, the disciple and interpreter of Peter, put into writing what Peter had preached. Luke, the follower of Paul, wrote down the gospel Paul preached. Lastly, John, the disciple of Jesus, set out the gospel while living at Ephesus.

Luke's Gospel – written about AD 80, probably for Christians at Caesarea by a Gentile (someone who was not a Jew).
It is likely that the writer was Luke, who travelled with Paul preaching about Jesus. Luke did not know Jesus but at the beginning of his gospel he says that he had made a close study of Jesus' life by talking to those who had known him.

John's Gospel – written AD 90–100, may have been written for Christians at Ephesus, possibly by someone who knew John the disciple of Jesus.
It is very unlikely that John wrote it himself – he would have been very old. In the gospel, John is described as the disciple 'Jesus loved most'. Is it likely that he would have described himself in this way?

B This small scrap of papyrus (early paper) was discovered in Egypt. In 1935 it was recognised as part of John's gospel (chapter 18, verses 31-3 on one side and verses 37-8 on the other). This copy of the gospel was made some time between AD 100 and 150 and it is the oldest copy of any of the gospels to have survived. It is shown here full size.

printing. Every copy had to be written out by hand.

2 News and information was passed on by word of mouth rather than in writing. The first Christians told people about Jesus by travelling around the country and preaching about him.

3 The first Christians were people who had known Jesus. Anyone who wanted to find out more about him could ask those who had known him. As the original disciples grew old it became more important to write down their memory of Jesus so that his life would not be forgotten.

4 Jesus' disciples may have thought that Jesus would return to them in their lifetimes. He had promised that he would return. They may not have felt the need to write a record of his life if he was coming back.

5 As the message of Christianity spread through the world it became increasingly important to have an account of Jesus' life and teaching written down.

It is possible that other books about Jesus were written before the gospels. If so, they have perished like most of the copy of John's gospel shown in **B**. Perhaps the gospel writers used earlier records when they wrote their books. What is clear is that by the time of Irenaeus, the four gospels of Matthew, Mark, Luke and John were accepted as the best account of Jesus' life and they are still the best evidence today.

❧❧ Things to do ❧❧

1 What does the word 'gospel' mean?

2 a) Add the writing of the gospels to your time chart.   b) Why were the events of Jesus' life not written down earlier?

3 a) Who does Irenaeus tell us wrote the gospels? b) How accurate was he in what he said about the gospel writers?

4 Do you think that any one gospel is likely to be more accurate than the others? Why?

Who Copied?

Have you ever copied anyone else's work at school? When the early Christians were writing about Jesus they did not think it was wrong to copy what someone else had written.

Look at **A**. It is the story of Jesus healing a man as told by Matthew, Mark and Luke. Read the three versions carefully.

Do you notice any similarities between the three passages? Read them again and make a list of words or phrases which appear in two or all three of the passages.

Matthew, Mark and Luke often record events in Jesus' life which John does not mention. Because they have a lot in common, these three gospels are called the *synoptic* gospels. This means that they present Jesus' life from a similar point of view. Sometimes whole sentences are exactly the same in these gospels. This is more than just coincidence. Why is there so much which is the same or nearly the same in the synoptic gospels?

Perhaps Matthew, Mark and Luke all copied from a book which is now lost. Perhaps one of the synoptic gospels was written first and the other two were copied from it. But which gospel was first and who copied?

Today most experts think that Mark wrote his gospel first and that Matthew and Luke used his as the basis of their own. The reasons why it is thought Matthew and Luke copied from Mark are listed in **B**.

 A

Mark 1, verses 40–45	Matthew 8, verses 1–4	Luke 5, verses 12–16
A man suffering from a dreaded skin-disease came to Jesus, knelt down, and begged him for help. 'If you want to,' he said, 'you can make me clean.' Jesus was filled with pity, and stretched out his hand and touched him. 'I do want to,' he answered. 'Be clean!' At once the disease left the man and he was clean. Then Jesus spoke sternly to him and sent him away at once, after saying to him, 'Listen, don't tell anyone about this. But go straight to the priest and let him examine you. Then in order to prove to everyone that you are cured, offer the sacrifice that Moses ordered.'	*When Jesus came down from the hill, large crowds followed him. Then a man suffering from a dreaded skin-disease came to him, knelt down before him, and said, 'Sir, if you want to, you can make me clean,' Jesus stretched out his hand and touched him. 'I do want to,' he answered. 'Be clean!' At once the man was healed of his disease. Then Jesus said to him, 'Listen! Don't tell anyone, go straight to the priest and let him examine you. Then in order to prove to everyone that you are cured, offer the sacrifice that Moses ordered.'*	*Once Jesus was in a town where there was a man suffering from a dreaded skin-disease. When he saw Jesus, he threw himself down and begged him, 'Sir, if you want to, you can make me clean!' Jesus stretched out his hand and touched him. 'I do want to,' he answered. 'Be clean!' At once the disease left the man. Jesus ordered him, 'Don't tell anyone, but go straight to the priest and let him examine you. Then to prove to everyone that you are cured, offer the sacrifice as Moses ordered.'*

B **1** Almost all the events recorded in Mark also appear in either Matthew or Luke and often in both. Mark consists of 661 verses and the events described in 631 of the verses are also described in the other two synoptic gospels.

2 Mark's version of the episodes in Jesus' life is usually longer than Matthew's or Luke's. The most likely explanation of this is that they *edited* and *compressed* Mark's gospel.

3 Both Matthew and Luke are longer than Mark overall. They include information about other events in Jesus' life which Mark does not mention.

It seems that Matthew and Luke 'improved' on what they borrowed from Mark and added to his account. We do not know where they got their extra information, but a lot of it is what Jesus said when teaching people. Often both Matthew and Luke agree word for word about what Jesus said. So some people think that they used another common source as well as Mark's gospel. **C** is a diagram showing how Matthew and Luke based their gospels on Mark's, added stories of their own and used another common source. This is called 'Q' after the German word *quelle* which means 'source'.

A medieval picture of Matthew writing his gospel. All books had to be written out by hand. Printing was not invented until over 1400 years after Jesus' death.

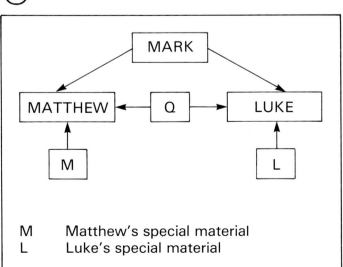

M   Matthew's special material
L   Luke's special material

❧ Things to do ❧

1 a) Why are the gospels of Matthew, Mark and Luke called the synoptic gospels? b) What is Q?

2 Look up the following passages in the Bible and make lists of the similarities between the three synoptic gospels: Mark 3, 13–19; Matthew 10, 1–4; Luke 6, 12–16. And, Mark 4, 35–41; Matthew 8, 18–27; Luke 8, 22–25;

3 From your comparison of the three passages in **A** say how convincing you think the evidence is to support the argument that Matthew and Luke copied from Mark.

The Jesus of the Gospels

Imagine if each person in your class were to write about someone you all knew. Would you all write the same things abut that person? Each of you would probably think of something different. You might all write something similar but it would not be the same.

If we look at the gospels, we find that each of the gospel writers presents Jesus in a different light. Look at **A**.

Why are the four gospel 'pictures' of Jesus different?

1 The gospel writers were relying on their own memories of Jesus or the memories of other people who knew him. Remember that the gospels were written at least thirty years after Jesus was killed.

2 The gospels were written for different kinds of reader. Matthew's references to Old

Mark's gospel concentrates on what Jesus did. He is shown as a man travelling around the country with a team of disciples healing the sick and working miracles. Mark's account of Jesus is lively and matter-of-fact giving an impression of someone who was active in the everyday world of his time.

In this gospel, other people claim Jesus is the Son of God but Jesus calls himself the Son of Man. Until his trial, he does not appear to make greater claims about himself.
Jesus asked his disciples 'Tell me, who do people say I am?' 'Some say that you are John the Baptist,' they answered. 'Others say that you are Elijah, while others say that you are one of the prophets.' 'What about you?' he asked them. 'Who do you say I am?' Peter answered, 'You are the Messiah.' Then Jesus ordered them, 'Do not tell anyone about me.'

Mark 8, 27–30

Matthew shows Jesus as a great teacher as well as a man of action. This gospel has five sections that are not in Mark which present Jesus teaching people how to lead a good life. The best known of these is the Sermon on the Mount (Matthew 5–7).

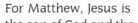

For Matthew, Jesus is the son of God and the Messiah (the Saviour whom the Jews believed God would send to rule them). Matthew often quotes from the Old Testament to show how Jesus' life and work was predicted to the Jews in the past.

As in Mark's gospel, Jesus calls himself the Son of Man. But Matthew presents him making definite claims to be the Son of God. When Jesus asks his disciples who they think he is, Matthew's version of the event is a bit different from Mark's.
Simon Peter answered, 'You are the Messiah, the Son of the living God.' 'Good for you, Simon son of John!' answered Jesus. 'For this truth did not come to you from any human being, but it was given to you directly by my Father in heaven.'... Then Jesus ordered his disciples not to tell anyone that he was the Messiah.

Matthew 16, 16–20

Testament prophecies suggest that he was writing for Jews who would know the Old Testament well.

3. The gospel writers wanted to convince people that Jesus was special, that he was the Son of God. Perhaps they did not just record what they remembered or found out about Jesus. They may also have interpreted Jesus' life in the light of what they later thought to be true.

❧ Things to do ❧

1 a) Which gospel was written for a Jewish readership? b) Which event is mentioned in all four gospels? c) Which gospel shows that Jesus cares for everyone?

2 Is it possible to say that any one of the four gospels gives the best and most accurate account of Jesus' life? Give reasons for your answer.

3 Do you think it would be possible to put the four gospels together to create a 'perfect' gospel giving a full description of Jesus' life and work? What problems might we have in doing this?

Luke presents Jesus as the friend of all people. A lot of the events in the life of Jesus which are only mentioned in Luke's gospel show Jesus helping people who were disliked, disapproved of or thought to be inferior by society at that time – foreigners, wrong-doers, criminals and the poor.

Women are also important friends of Jesus in Luke's gospel. In the time of Jesus, women did not have an important place in society but Luke mentions occasions when Jesus helped women. Jesus is shown to have equal concern for women as well as men.

Luke records more parable stories Jesus told than the other gospel writers. These parables are used to show how the disciples should behave. Those which are unique to this gospel stress kindness and caring for people. The most famous of the parables in Luke is the story of the Good Samaritan (see pages 32–3).

Luke calls Jesus 'King' and 'Lord'. For Luke, Jesus is the Messiah who has come to save all people, rich and poor, male and female, Jew and foreigner.

John describes some events which also occur in the other gospels – the events from the last week of Jesus' life and the feeding of the 5000 which appears in all four gospels. But most of what John tells us about Jesus is only found in his gospel.

For John, Jesus had human emotions and feelings, yet equally he was the unique Son of God. John shows us a Jesus who stresses his special role in his teaching and by his actions. Rather than just recording what Jesus said and did, John concentrates on the meaning and importance of Jesus' life. There are few parable stories in John's gospel. Jesus tells people about God and presents himself as the Son of God in a direct and powerful way. When he brings a friend, Lazarus, back from the dead, Jesus tells Lazarus' sister – *'I am the resurrection and the life. Whoever believes in me will live, even though he dies. And whoever lives and believes in me will never die. Do you believe this?' 'Yes, Lord!' she answered. 'I do believe that you are the Messiah, the Son of God, who was to come into the world.'*

John 11, 25–7

Where Jesus Lived

Do you think people from the south or north of Britain speak with a funny accent? Whichever accent you find strange probably depends on where you come from.

A is a map of the country Jesus lived in. He was brought up in Galilee, at Nazareth, in the north. Galileans were Jews but they spoke with a different accent from the main group of Jews who lived in Judaea further south. Matthew says that Peter's accent gave him away as a Galilean when he denied knowing Jesus.

In Jesus' time, the Jews in Galilee were separated from Judaea by the country of Samaria. Both the Galileans and the Judaeans did not like the Samaritans. Also, on the north, east and west, Galilee was surrounded by people who were not Jews. (Jews called non-Jewish people *Gentiles*).

Amongst Jews, Galileans had the reputation of being independent people. All of the countries on map **A** were part of the Roman Empire. Galileans were famous for their strong opposition to Roman rule.

Galilee was fertile and wealthy. **B** is Josephus' description of the region.

B *Galilee is so rich in soil and pasture and such a great number of trees grow there that even the laziest people are encouraged to be farmers.*

In particular, Galilee was famous for the grain, fruit and olives grown there and for the fish caught in the sea of Galilee. **C** and **D** show Galilee today.

Jesus' home town was Nazareth, but he travelled around the region a lot and spent some time living at Capernaum. Both these places were small country towns. The gospel writers hardly ever mention the big cities in the area. They present Jesus as a country person.

Many of the people Jesus taught would have been country people – fishermen, shepherds and farmers. To help them understand his message, Jesus illustrated his stories with examples from country life. He mentions everyday occupations like sowing seeds or

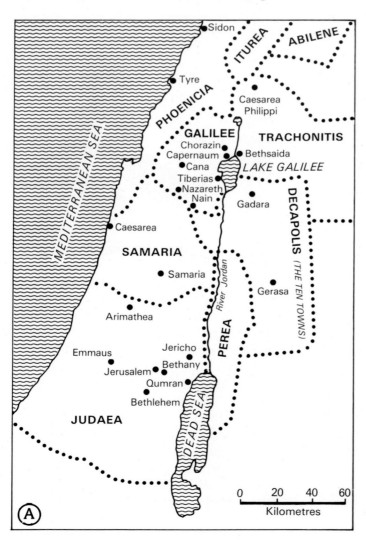

C

D

growing vines. He appreciates the beauty of the countryside. Read **E**.

(E) *Look at the birds flying around. They do not sow seeds, gather a harvest and put it in barns. Yet your Father in heaven takes care of them! Aren't you worth much more than birds? Can any of you live a bit longer by worrying about it? And why worry about clothes? Look how the wild flowers grow. They do not work or make clothes for themselves. But I tell you that not even King Soloman with all his wealth had clothes as beautiful as one of these flowers.* Matthew 6, 26–30

❧ Things to do ❧

1 a) Look at **A**. What are the names of the countries which border Galilee to the north, east and west? b) What was the difference between the people who lived in these countries and those who lived in Galilee and Judaea?

2 In his life and teaching, how did Jesus reflect the region he came from?

3 Why might Jesus have been disliked by the Jews in Judaea because he came from Galilee?

15

An Occupied Country

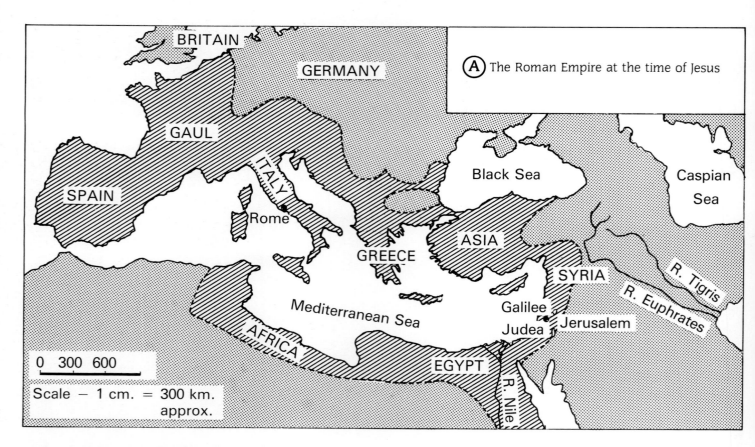

Map labels: BRITAIN, GERMANY, GAUL, ITALY, SPAIN, Rome, Black Sea, Caspian Sea, ASIA, GREECE, SYRIA, R. Tigris, R. Euphrates, Mediterranean Sea, Galilee, Judea, Jerusalem, AFRICA, EGYPT, R. Nile

0 300 600

Scale — 1 cm. = 300 km. approx.

How would you feel if armies from Russia or America invaded Britain?

Jesus' country had been invaded by the Romans in 63 BC. It was still occupied by the Romans during Jesus' life. **A** shows how large the Roman Empire was when Jesus was alive. Soldiers were stationed in Judaea and the Jews had to pay Roman taxes and obey Roman laws. But was Roman rule all that bad?

The Romans brought law and order to their empire. People could travel freely throughout the Mediterranean and trade flourished. In some ways the Romans treated the Jews better than they treated other conquered people. The Jews were allowed to have their own king and to practice their own religion. This was very important to them.

There was trouble though. Many Jews hated Roman rule and sometimes they revolted against it. One revolt against Rome took place when Jesus was a boy. It started in Jesus' home area, Galilee. This revolt began because the Romans had a *census* in AD 6 to see how much tax the Jews should pay to Rome. For many Jews the payment of tax to Rome which was ruled by a pagan Roman emperor (see **B**) was completely wrong. Under a leader called Judas the Galilean many Jews fought against Rome. The revolt was quashed but the group which Judas started survived. This group was called *Zealots* (which means dagger-men). One of Jesus' disciples may have been a Zealot.

D A Roman coin from the time of Jesus. The inscription means 'The God Augustus, Father'. Can you think why such an inscription would annoy the Jews?

There was more trouble between the Jews and the Romans some years after Jesus' death. In AD 70, there was another revolt. This time the Romans stamped out the opposition ruthlessly. They destroyed the Temple in Jerusalem which was the most holy of all Jewish places. The Jews had many of their rights taken away and a lot of them left Judaea to live elsewhere. It was at this time that the gospels were being written. Perhaps the early Christians, many of whom were Jews, wanted to play down any conflict there may have been between Jesus and the Romans so that they did not get into trouble.

B

How did Jesus feel about Roman rule? There is no evidence in the gospels to show that he was against it. Once some Jews asked Jesus a trick question to find out what he thought about the Romans. Read **C**.

C *'Is it against our Law for us to pay taxes to the Roman Emperor, or not?' But Jesus saw through their trick and said to them, 'Show me a silver coin. Whose face and name are these on it?' 'The Emperor's,' they answered. So Jesus said, 'Well, then, pay the Emperor what belongs to the Emperor, and pay God what belongs to God.'* Luke 20, 22–5

D shows a Roman coin like the one Jesus looked at. Jesus knew that he should be careful of what he said. If he had said it was wrong to pay Roman taxes he would have been in trouble with the Romans. After all he came from Galilee where trouble had started before. In his answer, Jesus refused to commit himself to either side.

⋙ Things to do ⋘

1 a) What happened in 63 BC? b) What happened in AD 70? c) Why did the events of AD 6 lead to a revolt against the Romans?

2 Look at **A**. Find the same area in a modern atlas and make a list of all the countries that were ruled by the Romans in the time of Jesus.

3 a) Give two reasons why Jesus might have been suspected of being anti-Roman. b) Explain why the gospel account of Jesus' attitude towards the Romans might be biased.

4 Imagine your country has been occupied by foreign rulers. How would you feel? Would you oppose the new rulers or try to go along with them?

Jesus and the Synagogue

The special building where Christians meet for worship is called a church. The place where Jews meet is called a *synagogue*, (a word which means 'gathered together'). Jesus was brought up a Jew and the synagogue played an important part in his life.

A shows the ruins of the synagogue at Capernaum. **B** shows the layout of a synagogue. In the middle is a raised platform where the president of the synagogue stands to lead the prayers. At the far end is a cupboard called an Ark. Inside are the handwritten scrolls (see **C**) which contain the Jewish scriptures.

Like all Jewish boys Jesus would have attended the synagogue on the Sabbath day. This is the Jewish holy day and it lasts from Friday evening until Saturday evening. On the Sabbath Jews do no work. They visit the synagogue, say prayers and eat special meals. Jesus probably went to Sabbath school to learn about the Jewish Law and scriptures.

Any adult Jewish man was allowed to teach in the synagogue and *interpret* (explain) the scriptures. So the synagogue was an obvious place for Jesus to start his teaching. At first, people probably thought he was just a clever young man. But the gospels suggest that there was something different about Jesus' teaching. Read **D**.

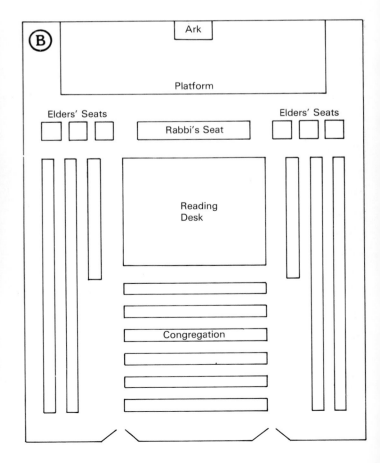

D *Jesus and his disciples came to the town of Capernaum, and on the next Sabbath Jesus went to the synagogue and began to teach. The people who heard him were amazed at the way he taught, for he wasn't like the teachers of the Law. Instead he taught with authority.* Mark 1, 21–2

Jesus became famous, especially when people heard of his power to heal illnesses. Read **E**.

E *Jesus went all over Galilee, teaching in the synagogues, preaching the Good News about the Kingdom, and healing people who had all kinds of disease and sickness. The news about him spread through the whole country of Syria, so that people brought to him all those who were sick, suffering from all kinds of diseases and disorders . . . and Jesus healed them all.* Matthew 4, 23–4

How do you think the elders and leaders of the synagogue felt about this new teacher from Nazareth? Later on, Jesus seems to have preached out-of-doors rather than in the synagogue. Perhaps he was not welcome in the synagogue or perhaps the crowds who wanted to hear him were too large to fit in the building.

Did Jesus intend to set himself apart from the Jewish religion and the traditions of the synagogue? In all four gospels he often refers to Old Testament writings, psalms and prophets. His audience would have expected this from a teacher. According to Matthew, Jesus saw himself continuing the Jewish traditions. Read **F**.

F *'Do not think that I have come to do away with the Law of Moses and the teachings of the prophets. I have not come to do away with them, but to make their teachings come true.'* Matthew 5, 17

C

In Luke, Jesus seems to mark a break with the Jewish religion. Read **G**.

G *The Law of Moses and the writings of the prophets were in effect up to the time of John the Baptist. Since then the Good News about the Kingdom of God is being told.* Luke 16, 16

Jewish scriptures said that a Messiah or Saviour would come. Jesus' followers may have seen him as the fulfilment of this prophecy, but Jesus might have seen himself as simply continuing the Jewish traditions.

❧ Things to do ❧

1 a) What is the Christian equivalent of the synagogue called? b) Look at **C**. What is the Christian equivalent of the Jewish scrolls called?

2 a) Why do you think Jesus started teaching in synagogues? b) Why might he have done most of his teaching out-of-doors later on?

3 In what ways do the gospels suggest Jesus' teaching was different? What do you think his listeners thought of him?

4 Try and find out if there is a synagogue in your town. If so, find out as much as you can about it. Perhaps your teacher could arrange a visit there.

Pharisees and Sadducees

There were two powerful religious groups among the Jews called the Pharisees and Sadducees. Jesus seems to have been very outspoken in criticising them, although he must have known that this would make him enemies.

The Pharisees

The word Pharisee means 'separated one'. Pharisees came from among the well-off business people and merchants. They believed they were better than other people. They kept themselves apart from Gentiles (non-Jews) and sinners. **A** is part of a notice forbidding non-Jews to enter the Temple in Jerusalem. The Pharisees were shocked by the sort of people Jesus associated with. Read **B**.

(B) *While Jesus was having a meal in Matthew's house, many tax collectors and other outcasts came and joined Jesus and his disciples at the table. Some Pharisees saw this and asked his disciples, 'Why does your teacher eat with such people?' Jesus heard them and answered, 'People who are well do not need a doctor, but only those who are sick.*

. . . I have not come to call respectable people, but outcasts.' Matthew 9, 10–13

The Pharisees lived by a strict code of behaviour. This was based on the Jewish Law and scriptures, and on traditions and rules which had grown up over the years. They had rules about what people should and should not do on the Sabbath day. Sometimes Jesus and his disciples openly broke these rules. Read **C**.

(C) *Jesus was walking through some cornfields on the Sabbath. His disciples began to pick some ears of corn, rub them in their hands and eat the grain. Some Pharisees asked, 'Why are you doing what our Law says you cannot do on the Sabbath?' Jesus answered them, 'Haven't you read what David did when he and his men were hungry? He went into the house of God, took the bread offered to God, ate it, and gave it also to his men. Yet it is against our Law for anyone except the priests to eat that bread.'* Luke 6, 1–4

This was a clever answer. The Pharisees prided themselves on their knowledge of the Law, but Jesus quoted the scriptures back at them. In the gospels he often criticizes them for their *hypocrisy*.

The Pharisees believed in life after death and a final judgement day. They also believed that a Messiah or Saviour would come, as the scriptures said. But many of them were horrified that a man like Jesus – a carpenter's son who went about with sinners and broke the laws – could be seen as the Messiah. They accused Jesus of *blasphemy*.

The Sadducees

The Sadducees came mainly from the well-off priestly families of Jerusalem. They were very powerful. Many of them held important positions in the *Sanhedrin*, the Jewish council which controlled Jerusalem and the surrounding area. This council dealt with religious problems, collected taxes, and served as a law court. The Sanhedrin could even sentence people to death if the Roman governor agreed. (Some Pharisees were also members of the Sanhedrin.) Unlike most other Jews, the Sadducees supported Roman rule. It protected their powerful position.

The Sadducees' religious beliefs were based strictly on the first five books of the Old Testament. They accepted no additions or changes to the Law contained in these books. They did not believe in life after death or in the coming of the Messiah. Josephus says about them –

(D) *They believe that man has the free choice of good or evil, and that it rests with each man's will whether he follows the one or the other. As for the survival of the soul after death, punishments in the underworld and rewards, they will have none of them.*

On one occasion, the Sadducees tried to trick Jesus with a question about the resurrection of the dead. Read **E**.

(E) *'Moses said that if a man who has no children dies, his brother must marry the widow so that they can have children who will be considered the dead man's children. Now, there were seven brothers who used to live here. The eldest got married and died without having children, so he left his widow to his brother. The same thing happened to the second brother, to the third, and finally to all seven. Last of all the woman died. Now, on the day when the dead rise to life, whose wife shall she be? All of them had married her.' Jesus answered them, 'How wrong you are! It is because you don't know the Scriptures or God's power. For when the dead rise to life, they will be like the angels in heaven and will not marry. Now, as for the dead rising to life, haven't you ever read what God has told you? He said, "I am the God of Abraham, the God of Isaac, and the God of Jacob." He is the God of the living, not of the dead.'* Matthew 22, 23–32

When Jesus was arrested (see pages 38–9) he was brought before the Sanhedrin for trial. The High Priest Caiaphas, a Sadducee, questioned him and found him guilty of blasphemy. The Sanhedrin then handed him over to the Roman governor to be condemned to death.

❧ Things to do ❧

1 Draw two columns. In one write down everything you know about the Pharisees. In the other write what you know about the Sadducees. In what ways were they similar? What were the differences between them?

2 Why do you think the Sadducees supported Roman rule while the Pharisees were against it?

3 From what you have read in this book, how would you expect, a) the Pharisees b) the Sadducees to have reacted to Jesus' teaching? Why might their feelings about Jesus have been dangerous for him?

John the Baptist

All four gospels begin the story of Jesus' adult life by describing his meeting with someone called John the Baptist. Who was John and why do all the gospels tell us about him?

John the Baptist was a holy man or prophet who drew large crowds to the wilderness of Judaea. His message was stern – *'Turn away from your sins because the Kingdom of heaven is near'*. John was a wild looking man. He dressed in a rough camel-skin robe tied with a leather belt. He lived on locusts (see **A**) and honey from wild bees.

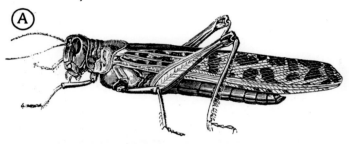

Ⓐ

John said that his followers must be baptized. He baptized them in the river Jordan (see **B**). The word *baptize* means 'to dip in water' and is a sign of being cleansed of sin. It shows a

Ⓑ

wish to make a fresh start in life. John baptized people by immersing them completely in water as sometimes happens today (see **C**).

John's call for people to turn away from sin was not new. It often occured in Jewish scriptures. Washing was an important part of Jewish ritual and the idea of baptism was not unusual either.

The gospel writers present John as more than just a Jewish holy man. He is a messenger from God sent to prepare people for the coming of Jesus. All the gospels say that John announced that someone greater would come after him. But did John recognise Jesus as the person he was expecting? The gospels present conflicting evidence. The accounts of Jesus' baptism by John are slightly different.

Mark describes the event quite simply. Read **E**.

Ⓔ *Jesus came from Nazareth in the province of Galilee, and was baptized by John in the Jordan. As soon as Jesus came up out of the water, he saw heaven opening and the Spirit coming down on him like a dove. And a voice came from heaven, 'You are my own dear Son. I am pleased with you.'*   Mark 1, 9–11

In this account there is no suggestion that John recognised Jesus or that anyone saw anything unusual in the baptism. The voice from heaven is addressed to Jesus rather than John or anyone else. What happened could have been a private emotional experience which Jesus later described to his disciples.

Matthew presents a different picture. Read **F**.

C

D

F *Jesus arrived from Galilee and came to John at the Jordan to be baptized by him. But John tried to make him change his mind. 'I ought to be baptized by you,' John said, 'and yet you have come to me!' But Jesus answered him, 'Let it be so for now. For in this way we shall do all that God requires.' So John agreed. As soon as Jesus was baptized, he came up out of the water. Then heaven was opened to him, and he saw the Spirit of God coming down like a dove and alighting on him. Then a voice said from heaven, 'This is my own dear Son, with whom I am pleased.'* Matthew 3, 13–17

Matthew's account shows John recognising Jesus as greater than himself. Also the voice from heaven does not address Jesus, but seems to be pointing him out to the onlookers. But Matthew also has evidence that John may not have been sure about who Jesus was.

Matthew tells us that when John was arrested by the ruler of Galilee, Herod Antipas, he sent some of his followers to Jesus with a message, **G**.

G *'Are you the one John said was going to come, or should we expect someone else?' Jesus answered, 'Go back and tell John what you are hearing and seeing: the blind can see, the lame can walk, those who suffer from dreaded skin-diseases are made clean, the deaf hear, the dead are brought back to life, and the Good News is preached to the poor. How happy are those who have no doubts about me!'* Matthew 11, 3–6

Was John asking for reassurance that Jesus really was the Messiah? Or did he want someone to get him out of prison? Jesus avoids answering the question directly. What did his answer mean?

⬦ **Things to do** ⬦

1 Look up Luke's and John's account of Jesus' meeting with John the Baptist, (Luke 3, 21–2 and John 1, 29–34). Make a list of the differences between the two accounts.
2 Imagine you have gone out into the wilderness to see John the Baptist. Write about what you see and hear. What does he look like? What do you think of him?
3 Why do you think people might want to be baptized by total immersion? What is the difference between the baptisms shown in **C** and **D**?

The Essenes

In 1947, an Arab goat boy discovered by accident some scrolls (**A**) in a cave by the Dead Sea (**B**). Historians think that these scrolls belonged to a group (or sect) of Jews called Essenes who lived a secluded life at the time of Jesus. This sect began in the second century BC but did not last after the second century AD. At the time of Jesus, there were about 4000 Essenes in Judaea. They may have hidden their scrolls when they were forced to escape from the Romans after the revolt by the Jews in AD 70. At this time the Romans destroyed everything connected with the Jewish religion and people.

In 1951, archaeologists found the remains of a monastery at Khirbet Qumran and experts think that the Essenes lived there. See **C**.

Josephus mentions the Essenes, (see **D**), but until the scrolls and the monastery were discovered, hardly anything was known about the sect.

Copper scrolls

Papyrus (paper) scrolls

C

(D) *The Essenes shun pleasure. Marriage they scorn. But they adopt other people's children while they are still pliable and docile and they regard them as their family and mould them in accordance with their own principles.*

Since John the Baptist's parents died early and he seems to show a similarity with the Essenes, could he have been adopted and brought up by them? What is more important for Christianity is whether Jesus could have been associated with the Essenes at some stage in his life.

The gospels never mention the Essenes but Jesus sometimes taught near the area where the Essenes lived. Could the Essene movement have influenced Jesus and John the Baptist in their thinking? **E** lists some of the similarities between Jesus, John the Baptist and the Essenes. Study it carefully.

Despite the similarities between Jesus, John the Baptist and the Essenes, there were many differences and historians today think that there was no link between them. But not all the scrolls have been studied. Perhaps there is more to be discovered.

What the scrolls do show is how Jesus was a man of his time in that some of the ideas he held were shared by other people within the Jewish religion.

(E)

	Jesus	John the Baptist	The Essenes
1	spent some time in the wilderness	lived for a time in the wilderness	lived by the Dead Sea in the wilderness
2		lived on locusts and wild honey	lived on food they grew
3	did not marry	did not marry	did not marry
4	held pacifist views	held pacifist views	held pacifist views
5	was baptized by John and baptism was later adopted by Christianity	practised baptism	practised baptism
6	chose 12 disciples		had the practice of having 12 people working together
7	had communal meals with his disciples		attached importance to a communal meal

⚶| Things to do |⚶

1 What is the difference between a scroll and a book?

2 Describe what you think life in the monastery at Khirbet Qumran was like. Why might the Essenes have chosen to live in the wilderness?

3 Look at the evidence in **E**. Do you think there was any connection between Jesus, John the Baptist and the Essenes? Give reasons for your answer.

4 What help is the evidence from the scrolls and the monastery in understanding Jesus?

Temptation

Was Jesus an ordinary man or was he special in some way? This is a question that people have often asked. In what way was he like other men, and equally, in what way was he considered special? Do we see two contrasting pictures of Jesus?

We know from the gospels that at one time Jesus spent six weeks in the wilderness. See **A**. We are told that here he was tempted by the devil three times. These temptations took place while he was trying to work out the nature of his future work. It was an important time for Jesus. He had to decide how to complete his work. We are told that he was visited by the devil and tempted but with each temptation he found guidance in the Jewish scriptures.

In the first temptation, the devil tempted Jesus to feed the many poor people of the land by turning stones into bread. Jesus turned the idea down, realizing that what people needed was a spiritual message. He quoted the Jewish scriptures in his reply. Read **B**.

B *Man must not depend on bread alone to sustain him, but on everything that the Lord says.*

Deuteronomy 8, 3

The second temptation suggested that Jesus jump from a pinnacle of the Temple in Jerusalem. If he could save himself, the people would think he had superhuman powers. In their eyes he would become a kind of wonder worker. **C** is a picture of a model of the Temple at this time. This will give you an idea of its height. Jesus again turned to Jewish scriptures for guidance. Read **D**.

D *Do not put the Lord your God to the test.*

Deuteronomy 6, 16

For his third temptation, the devil offered Jesus

power over all the kingdoms of the world if he would worship him. Jesus answered with another quotation. Read **E**.

E *Fear the Lord your God, worship only him.*

Deuteronomy 6, 13

Was Jesus rejecting earthly power and force in his reply?

Jesus must have told his disciples about these temptations. But did they really happen like this? In Jesus' time many people believed in the devil as a real force. Many people feel the same today, but many people also feel that temptations or doubts come from inside themselves. Perhaps the gospel account of the temptations should be understood in this way. Was Jesus having doubts about himself and what he could achieve?

Whatever happened in the wilderness, the temptations show Jesus as someone who could understand ordinary human doubts and weakness. They also show him as someone who was determined to live by God's law.

⊷≫| Things to do |⋘⊶

1 Make three columns in your book to describe the three temptations. In the first column, mention what the temptation was. In the second column, give Jesus' response, and in the third column write the name of the Old Testament book and chapter that Jesus quoted in his reply.

2 Do people believe in a devil today? What is another interpretation of the temptations?

3 Does the evidence suggest that Jesus regarded himself as special at this point in his life?

4 Read the story of the temptations in Matthew's gospel, chapter 4 verses 1 – 11. Why do you think Jesus went away on his own into the wilderness? Describe what it would have been like living in the wilderness for nearly six weeks. Do you think it would have been easy to resist the temptations?

The Disciples

Did you know that you are disciples? The word *disciple* means 'pupil' or 'learner' and you are disciples of your teacher. Jesus had disciples who often called him 'Rabbi' or 'Teacher'. He chose 12 people in particular to be his closest companions.

We know very little about the disciples apart from what the gospels tell us and they do not tell us much about anyone except Peter. Look at **A**. It is a famous painting of the last meal Jesus had with his disciples before he was killed with details about the disciples.

What sort of people were the disciples? From what we know they all seem ordinary people who were impressed by Jesus. When Jesus called them they left their work and their families to follow him. The disciples were all Jews, and, apart from Judas, they came from Galilee. Jesus had great plans for the work of his disciples. Read **B**.

B *'I have chosen you to be with me', he told them. 'I will also send you out to preach and you will have authority to drive out demons'.*

Mark 3, 14–15

The disciples did not always understand what Jesus told them but after his death they fearlessly went about telling people about him. The Jewish authorities were astonished by this. Read **C**.

C *The members of the Council were amazed to see how bold Peter and John were and to learn that they were ordinary men of no education. They realised then that they had been companions of Jesus.* Acts 4, 13

Bartholomew
Also called Nathaniel. Philip brought him to Jesus. At first Bartholomew was very doubtful about Jesus. 'Can anything good come from Nazareth?' he said, but he was won over. Bartholomew may have been killed in Armenia.

Bartholomew James Andrew Judas Pe

James the son of
Alphaeus. He was also called James the Less or James the Younger to distinguish him from the other James. Later tradition says that he was killed with a saw.

Andrew
Peter's brother, also a fisherman. According to John's gospel, Andrew was a disciple of John the Baptist before following Jesus. Andrew introduced Peter to Jesus. He may have been crucified in Greece on an X-shaped cross.

Judas Iscariot
The name Iscariot probably means the place Judas came from, Kerioth in Judaea. Judas was the treasurer of the disciples. John's gospel says he stole the money he was meant to be looking after. He betrayed Jesus to the Jewish authorities. Later he regretted this and committed suicide.

Peter
A fisherman from Bethsaida. He spoke with a strong Galilean accent because it was recognised in Jerusalem. Originally called Simon, Jesus gave him the name Peter and treated him as the leader of the disciples. Though Peter let Jesus down the night Jesus was arrested, Peter became one of the most important Christian leaders after Jesus' death. Tradition says that Peter was crucified upside down in Rome in about 64 AD.

Thomas

Also called Didymus which is a Greek word meaning 'twin'. Christians call him 'Doubting Thomas' because he did not believe in Jesus' resurrection until he touched the holes in Jesus' hands.

Philip

Jesus called Philip to join the disciples soon after Andrew and Peter. He came from Bethsaida. Philip may have died at a place called Hierapolis in Turkey.

Judas

Also called Thaddeus. Christian tradition says that Judas later became a missionary.

Matthew

A tax collector. He was also called Levi. The gospel of Matthew is attributed to him but experts question whether he wrote it.

Simon

Called Simon the Zealot which suggests that he may once have belonged to the Zealot party.

Thomas James   Philip   Matthew   Judas   Simon

John

He was a fisherman and, like Andrew, may have been a disciple of John the Baptist before meeting Jesus. Jesus called John and his elder brother, James, 'Sons of Thunder' because of their fiery natures.

In the fourth gospel, the disciple John is called 'the one Jesus loved most'.

James

John's elder brother. James is sometimes mentioned with Peter and John accompanying Jesus when the other disciples were not present. James was also a fisherman. Herod Agrippa I had James beheaded in about AD 44.

✥ Things to do ✥

1 a) Which was the disciple that Jesus loved most? b) Who was the leader of the disciples? c) Who were the 'Sons of Thunder'? d) Which disciple betrayed Jesus? e) Which disciple doubted the resurrection at first?

2 Why do you think Jesus chose disciples? What qualities might he have looked for in the people he picked?

3 What kind of followers might Jesus choose if he were alive today? Would some of them be women? What sort of jobs might they do?

Miraculous Happenings

Do you believe in miracles? At Lourdes in France today, it is claimed that many healings of sick and disabled people take place. It is said that these people are healed because of their great faith that Jesus will heal them. But can someone really be healed like this?

Was Jesus a faith healer? Josephus describes Jesus as a 'wonder-worker' and the gospels show him doing things which people thought were miracles.

How should we explain the miracles in the gospels? Study **A** to **C** which are shortened accounts of three miracles of Jesus.

Did these miracles really happen like this? What other explanations are there for these events? Could Jesus have had special medical knowledge? Were the people 2000 years ago more easily fooled than we are?

It is impossible to know exactly what happened when Jesus performed a miracle. At the time many people thought Jesus had special powers and crowds flocked to see him.

There were other wonder-workers active in Jesus' time. They wanted to show others their great powers. In contrast to them, Jesus tried to keep his activities a secret. He did not want Jairus' family telling people what he had done. Jesus is shown to be aware that his miracles were a sign of being the Messiah but he refused to demonstrate his power just to please others.

Mosaic of the healing of Jairus' daughter, AD 1320

A Jewish leader called Jairus begged Jesus to heal his daughter. Jesus went to his house and found the girl dead. He took hold of the girl's hand and told her to get up. She got up immediately and started to walk. Everyone was absolutely amazed. Jesus gave strict orders to the family not to tell anyone about this.
Mark 5, 21–24, 35–43

Flat roofed houses in Israel today.

Mosaic of the feeding of the 5000, about AD 520

When Jesus was at Capernaum in Galilee, a crowd collected at the door of the house where he was staying. There were so many people there that four men decided to carry a paralysed friend up to the roof and let him down through an opening. Jesus was so impressed with their faith that he healed the man immediately. Mark 2, 1–5

One day when Jesus was busy teaching the people new things, his disciples suggested he send people away to buy food. Jesus said they must all be given something to eat. The disciples only had 5 loaves and 2 fishes but when Jesus distributed this there was found to be enough to feed 5000 people. John 6,1–11

❧ Things to do ☙

1 a–d are possible explanations of what happened at the feeding of the 5000. Which do you think is the best explanation? Why?
a) Jesus actually created enough food from 2 loaves and 5 fishes to feed 5000 people. b) When people saw Jesus sharing out food they shared what they had brought with them. c) Jesus fed peoples' minds with his teaching and the loaves and fishes were signs that the people felt well fed. d) The gospel writers made up the story to show how great they thought Jesus was.
Can you think of any other explanations for what happened?

2 Why do you think Jesus wanted to keep his miracles secret? Why might the people he healed have wanted to tell everyone?

3 Imagine you were a newspaper reporter present at one of the events **A–C**. Write a report about what happened. Think up a good headline and try and explain what Jesus did and the way the crowds reacted. Use the pictures to help you describe the scene.

Jesus the Teacher

Do you like hearing stories? Does your teacher ever tell you stories? Would you pay more attention in class if your teacher told you a good story?

In Jesus' time people were used to listening to story-tellers since hardly anything was written down and not many people could read. Jesus seems to have been a good story-teller. Many of his followers would have been uneducated people and Jesus often used stories to get his message across.

In the Bible, Jesus' stories are called *parables*. This is a word that describes a story with some special meaning or message in it.

A lawyer once asked Jesus the question *'Who is my neighbour?'* and Jesus replied with a story. Read **A**.

(A) *'There was once a man who was going down from Jerusalem to Jericho when robbers attacked him, stripped him and beat him up, leaving him half dead. It so happened that a priest was going down that road but when he saw the man he walked on by, on the other side. In the same way a Levite also came along, went over and looked at the man, and then walked on by, on the other side. But a Samaritan who was travelling that way came upon the man, and when he saw him, his heart was filled with pity. He went over to him, poured oil and wine on his wounds and bandaged them. Then he put the man on his own animal and took him to an inn, where he took care of him. The next day he took out two silver coins and gave them to the innkeeper. "Take care of him," he told the innkeeper,*

(B)

"and when I come back this way, I will pay you whatever else you spend on him."' And Jesus concluded, 'In your opinion, which one of these three acted like a neighbour towards the man attacked by the robbers?' The teacher of the Law answered, 'The one who was kind to him.' Jesus replied, 'You go, then, and do the same.'

Luke 10, 29–37

Jesus' message of caring for those who suffer appeals to everyone who hears this story. In his own day this story would have had special force. His audience might have known the wild road from Jerusalem to Jericho (**B**) and the lonely inn on the way like the one in **C**. They would have been able to *identify* with the wounded traveller (imagine themselves in his place). So they would have been very shocked when Jesus chose a Samaritan for the 'hero' of his story. The Jews disliked the Samaritans.

(C)

Although Samaritans were Jews, their religious practice was different and strict Jews treated them as outcasts. They would not willingly let themselves be touched by a Samaritan. But the Samaritan in the story does more than either of the Jews. This would have shocked Jesus' Jewish audience.

Jesus wanted his audience to think about the meaning of his story. By chosing a Samaritan as the person who acts best he *challenges* his audience's beliefs and *prejudices*. By telling this story, Jesus made his point much more powerfully than if he had just said 'Everyone is your neighbour' in answer to the lawyer's question.

The gospels show Jesus as a good teacher. His disciples often called him 'Rabbi'. This name means teacher and was a mark of respect for someone who was worth listening to. Jesus understood how to get his point across to all kinds of people, ordinary people or clever people like the lawyer. There seems to have been something special about Jesus which compelled people to listen to him (**D**).

(**D**) *When Jesus finished saying these things, the crowd was amazed at the way he taught. He was not like the teachers of the Law. Instead he taught with authority.*

Matthew 7, 28–9

❧| Things to do |❧

1 a) What is Jesus' message in the story of the good Samaritan?   b) Why did Jesus choose a Samaritan for the hero of his story?   c) Why do you think Jesus chose a priest as the first person to discover the wounded man on the road to Jericho?

2 a) Why do you think the priest left the wounded man lying on the side of the road?   b) Imagine you were the wounded man. What would have been your feelings as you lay in the road after being attacked? Write about your ordeal describing what happened and what you felt.

3 Why do you think Jesus told stories to get his message across?

A New Religion?

Did Jesus want to start a new religion? In Matthew's gospel Jesus says,

A *'I have been sent only to those lost sheep, the people of Israel.'*   Matthew 15, 24

The Jews were the 'people of Israel'. Does this mean that Jesus, who was a Jew, was only interested in teaching the Jews?

All Jesus' disciples were Jews and most of the people he met and talked to were Jews. But Jesus did travel through Gentile (non-Jewish) areas and he seems to have treated all people equally. To very religious Jews like the Pharisees and Sadducees, all people were not equal. These strict Jews despised both those who were not Jewish and those Jews who did not keep to the strict rules of the Jewish religion. **B** is a story Luke tells which shows the difference between Jesus and a Pharisee called Simon.

B *A Pharisee invited Jesus to have dinner with him, and Jesus went to his house and sat down to eat. In that town was a woman who lived a sinful life. She heard that Jesus was eating in the Pharisee's house, so she brought an alabaster jar full of perfume and stood behind Jesus, by his feet, crying and wetting his feet with her tears. Then she dried his feet with her hair, kissed them, and poured the perfume on them. When the Pharisee saw this, he said to himself, 'If this man really were a prophet, he would know who this woman is who is touching him. He would know what kind of sinful life she lives!' . . .*

Then Jesus turned to the woman and said to Simon, 'Do you see this woman? I came into your home, and you gave me no water for my feet, but she has washed my feet with her tears and dried them with her hair. You did not welcome me with a kiss, but she has not stopped kissing my feet since she came. You provided no olive-oil for my head, but she has covered my feet with perfume. I tell you, then, the great love she has shown proves that her many sins have been forgiven. But whoever has been forgiven little shows only a little love.'   Luke 7, 36–9, 44–7

It was normal for a host to welcome his guests with a kiss, to provide water for washing and to anoint them with oil. The Pharisee had not done these things. The woman's behaviour showed that she was sorry for her sins.

Throughout the gospels we are shown that Jesus did not *discriminate* amongst the people he met (that means he treated them all equally). He was ready to eat with tax-collectors, wrong-doers – and Pharisees. He cured lepers and beggars – as well as the daughter of Jairus, President of the Synagogue. But as the story of Jesus' visit to Simon the Pharisee's house shows, this lack of discrimination made him unpopular with many other Jews.

C is a table listing some of the Gentiles and sinners Jesus met and helped.

D is a map showing Gentile areas (shaded) and Jewish areas (not shaded).

C	Woman from Tyre	Jesus cured her daughter of a demon	*Mark 7, 24–30*
	A Roman army officer	Jesus cured his sick servant	*Luke 7, 1–10*
	Man from Gerasa	Cured of demons	*Luke 8, 26–39*
	Zacchaeus	A tax-collector Jesus wanted to visit for dinner	*Luke 19, 1–10*
	Woman condemned for adultery	Saved from being punished	*John 8, 1–11*
	Samaritan woman	Jesus offered her life-giving water	*John 4, 1–30*

D

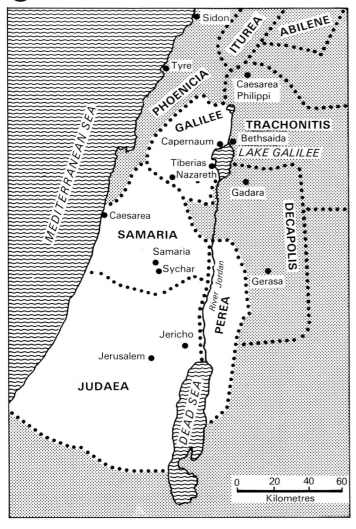

❧ Things to do ❧

1 a) Who were the 'lost sheep of the house of Israel'? b) Why did Simon criticise Jesus? c) How did the sinful woman show her love for Jesus? d) How did Simon welcome Jesus? e) Do you think Simon liked Jesus?

2 Can you work out why a strict Jew would have despised the 6 people in **C**? Use the map **D** to help you.
a) Woman from Tyre b) Roman army officer (Clue – see page 22) c) Man from Gerasa d) Zacchaeus (Clue – see page 22) e) Woman condemned for adultery f) Samaritan woman (Clue – see page 32)

3 Copy the map **D** and colour it in or shade it to distinguish Gentile areas from Jewish areas.

4 What is the link between Jesus' attitude to people and the starting of Christianity as a new religion?

One Week in a Short Life

From the evidence of the four gospels it seems that Jesus spent the last week of his life in Jerusalem. Christians call this Holy Week. The gospels record the events of these few days in detail but we cannot be sure that all of them actually took place in the same week. Perhaps the gospel writers concentrated events in Jesus' life into one week to build up the story before his death.

The events of the last week are set at the time of the Passover when Jews celebrated the time when their ancestors escaped from slavery in Egypt. This festival took place in April. As a practising Jew, Jesus travelled to Jerusalem for the festival. Most pilgrims walked to the city, but Jesus arrived in an unusual way, riding on a donkey, and he attracted a lot of attention, (**A** and **B**).

(**A**) *A large crowd of people spread their cloaks on the road while others cut branches from the trees and spread them on the road. The crowds walking in front of Jesus and those walking behind began to shout, 'Praise to David's Son! God bless him who comes in the name of the Lord! Praise God!'*
When Jesus entered Jerusalem, the whole city was thrown into an uproar. 'Who is he?' the people asked. 'This is the prophet Jesus, from Nazareth in Galilee,' the crowds answered.

Matthew 21, 8–11

Why did Jesus choose to arrive in this spectacular way? Until this point Jesus seems to have avoided attracting too much attention. With his entry into Jerusalem this changed. Matthew tells us the city 'went wild' about him. Had events got out of hand or was Jesus

(**B**)

trying to provoke a show-down with the authorities? Both the Jewish and the Roman authorities must have been alarmed by the stir Jesus caused.

Matthew and John say that Jesus was fulfilling the words of an Old Testament prophet, Zechariah, **C**.

(**C**) *'Tell the city of Zion (Jerusalem), look, your king is coming to you! He is humble and rides on a donkey'*

Matthew 21, 5

This reference to the coming of a king would have been familiar to Jesus, his followers and to the Jewish authorities. Was Jesus claiming to be the Messiah, the forthcoming king?

D lists the main events in the week that followed. Notice how many times Jesus seems to have come into conflict with the authorities. On **E** you can see where some of the main events took place.

D THE LAST WEEK

Sunday   Jesus arrives in Jerusalem from Bethany. He is welcomed by cheering crowds.

Monday   Jesus goes to the Temple and violently turns out the money-lenders and tradesmen who had stalls there (**F**). (These men exchanged Roman money for special Temple Money which people used to buy animals to sacrifice at the Passover festival. The traders often made large profits.)

Tuesday   Jesus teaches in the Temple. He is questioned by: the Pharisees – about the authority for his teaching; Herod's followers – about paying taxes to Rome; the Sadducees – about resurrection. They try to catch Jesus out, but fail.

Wednesday   Judas Iscariot offers to betray Jesus to the Chief Priests for 30 pieces of silver. We are given no clues about why Judas does this.

Thursday   Jesus and the disciples eat their last meal together in an upper room in Jerusalem. Afterwards they go to the garden of Gethsemane. Here Judas betrays Jesus and he is arrested.

Friday   Jesus is tried, by the Jewish leaders at Caiaphas the High Priest's house, by Pilate at the Governor's residence and, according to Luke, by Herod at his palace in the Fortress of Antonia. Jesus is executed at Golgotha.

F

E Jerusalem in the Time of Jesus

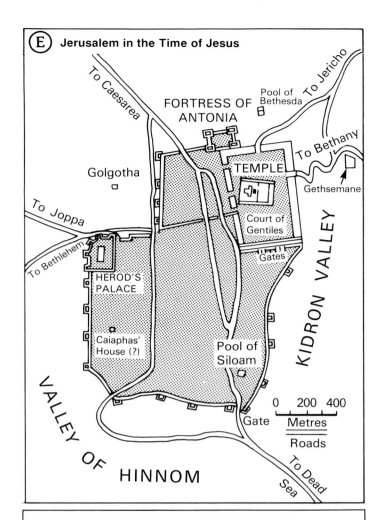

🌿 Things to do 🌿

1 Copy out the map of Jerusalem, **E** and mark on it the places mentioned in **D**.

2 a) What evidence can you find in this chapter which suggests that Jesus was trying to provoke the authorities? b) What evidence can you find which suggests that the authorities were worried about Jesus? The questions Jesus was asked on Tuesday are a clue.   c) Can you think of any reasons why Jesus wanted to cause a stir during the last week of his life?

3 B and F are pictures of two of the events mentioned in this chapter. Imagine you are a newspaper reporter. Describe one of these events.

The Last Night

Do you think 13 is an unlucky number? Many people do. Perhaps this superstition is because there were 13 people present at Jesus' last meal with his disciples. After the meal Jesus was arrested.

According to the gospel accounts, Jesus made arrangements in advance for this meal with his disciples. They ate in an upstairs room in a house in Jerusalem. (The house may have belonged to the family of the gospel-writer Mark.)

The disciples probably expected this to be no different from many other meals they had shared with Jesus. But that night he had a special message for them, **A**.

C

(A) *While they were at the table eating, Jesus said, 'I tell you that one of you will betray me – one who is eating with me.' The disciples were upset and began to ask him, one after the other, 'Surely you don't mean me, do you?' Jesus answered, 'It will be one of you twelve.'*
Mark 14, 18–20

Jesus also had another message for the disciples, **B**.

(B) *While they were eating, Jesus took a piece of bread, gave a prayer of thanks, broke it, and gave it to his disciples. 'Take it' he said, 'this is my body.' Then he took a cup, gave thanks to God, and handed it to them, and they all drank from it. Jesus said, 'This is my blood which is poured out for many.'* Mark 14, 22–24

The gospel writers present Jesus as knowing what was going to happen to him. He was warning his disciples that he would be be-trayed and killed. His body would be broken like the bread and his blood would be spilled like the wine. Today, Christians remember Jesus' words at this last meal during a special service called *Communion*. In this service the Christians present take a small portion of bread and a small sip of wine.

After the last supper, Jesus and the disciples went to a public place called the Garden of Gethsemane just outside Jerusalem (**C**). The gospel writers say that Jesus wanted to pray quietly by himself.

The disciple Judas must have known that Jesus would be alone at this time, away from the crowds that usually surrounded him. Judas led an armed guard, sent by the Jewish authorities, to the garden to arrest Jesus. Judas showed who Jesus was by going up to him and kissing him. Jesus did not put up a fight. The disciples ran away and Jesus was arrested and taken for trial.

It is difficult to be sure how many trials Jesus had, though it seems he was questioned by both the Jews and the Romans. The gospels give slightly different accounts of what happened, but this is the time-table that appears if we put them all together:

10pm Before Annas (John)

Jesus was first taken to Annas, father-in-law of the High Priest Caiaphas.

11pm Before Caiaphas (John)

Caiaphas may have interrogated Jesus while the Jewish Council was assembling.

4am Before the Sanhedrin (Mark, Matthew and Luke)

The whole Sanhedrin, or Jewish Council, assembled to try Jesus. They wanted his death. They brought witnesses to speak against him but their evidence did not agree. The Council accused Jesus of blasphemy and they had the power to try religious offences. But the Jewish Council could not condemn anyone to death. Only the Romans could do that. So the Jews took Jesus to the Roman authorities.

6am Before Pilate (Luke)

Jesus was brought before Pontius Pilate, the Roman governor of Judaea and Samaria (AD 26–36). The Jews accused Jesus of claiming to be king but Pilate could find nothing to charge Jesus with. Hearing that Jesus came from Galilee, Pilate sent him to see Herod Antipas, the governor of that area. Herod was in Jerusalem at the time.

7am Before Herod Antipas (Luke)

Like Pilate, Herod could find no evidence to condemn Jesus. He and his men thought Jesus was a 'joke' and they made cruel fun of him before sending him back to Pilate.

8am Before Pilate (All four gospels)

This was Jesus' last trial and the four gospels give similar accounts of what happened. **D** is Luke's version.

D *Pilate called together the chief priests, the leaders and the people, and said to them, 'You brought this man to me and said that he was misleading the people. Now, I have examined him here in your presence, and I have not found him guilty of any of the crimes you accuse him of. Nor did Herod find him guilty, for he sent him back to us. There is nothing this man has done to deserve death. So I will have him whipped and let him go.' The whole crowd cried out, 'Kill him!'*   Luke 23, 13–18

Pilate gave in to the crowd's wishes.

❧ Things to do ❧

1 a) Which one of the disciples might have felt uneasy at the last supper? Why? b) At the last supper what did Jesus say was going to happen to him?   c) What is the connection between **B** and the Communion service?

2 a) Why do you think Jesus' arrest took place in the garden of Gethsemane? b) Why did the Sanhedrin send Jesus to the Roman governor to be tried?   c) Why did Pontius Pilate send Jesus to Herod Antipas?

3 When he was on trial before the Sanhedrin, Jesus was accused of *religious offences* but when he was brought before Pilate he was accused of a *civil offence*, of claiming to be king. Why do you think his accusers changed the charge against him?

Was Jesus a Criminal?

On the previous page we saw that Jesus was condemned to death. What was his crime that he was punished like this? The gospels present Jesus as being innocent of any crime. So why did the crowd around Pilate call for Jesus' death? Why did Pilate agree to his execution? Did Pilate really believe Jesus was innocent as the gospels claim?

If we look at the background to the trial and read between the lines of the gospel record it is possible to understand some of the reasons Jesus was executed. To get a fair picture we must consider the evidence from all the points of view of those involved, from the Jewish, the Roman and the Christian points of view.

❦❦ Things to do ❦❦

1 a) What was Jesus' crime from the Jewish point of view? b) Why might the Romans have been worried about Jesus?

2 Do you think the Jews had a convincing case against Jesus? From what you have read about the Jewish religion give reasons for your answer.

3 There are no detailed records of Jesus' trial from a Jewish or a Roman point of view. We only have the gospel account. Why might the gospels not present a fair account of what happened?

4 Compare Matthew's account of Jesus' trial before the Sanhedrin (**A**) with Mark's account (Mark 14, 61–4). Why do you think they are different? Does Mark's account alter your view about why Jesus was condemned? Why?

THE JEWISH POINT OF VIEW

The Talmud, a Jewish book written in the second century AD, refers to Jesus as a criminal who was justly tried and executed. The gospels present Jesus as being in conflict with the Jewish authorities.

The Jews' Case Against Jesus

- Jesus said he could forgive sins. The Jews believed that only God had the power to forgive sins. Jesus' claim outraged them.
- Jesus offended the Jews by eating and drinking with sinners – people the Jews said were unclean.
- Jesus broke the Sabbath law by healing people on the Sabbath. The Jews said this was working on the Sabbath which was prohibited.
- Jesus publicly criticised the Pharisees and Sadducees.
- The Jews believed that Jesus was guilty of blasphemy because he claimed to be the Messiah. They accused him of this at his trial, see **A**.

Ⓐ *The High Priest spoke to him, 'In the name of the living God I now put you on oath. Tell us if you are the Messiah, the Son of God.' Jesus answered him, 'So you say. But I tell all of you, from this time on you will see the Son of Man sitting on the right of the Almighty and coming on the clouds of heaven!' At this the High Priest tore his clothes and said, 'Blasphemy! We don't need any more witnesses! You have just heard his blasphemy! What do you think?' They answered, 'He is guilty and must die.'*
Matthew 26, 63–6

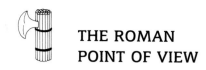

THE ROMAN
POINT OF VIEW

There is no evidence in the gospels that Jesus actively opposed Roman rule. In fact, this is something that many Jews may have held against him. Some people think that Judas hoped Jesus would lead an armed revolt against the Romans and betrayed Jesus because he was disappointed that this did not happen. The Romans might have seen Jesus as a threat however.

The Romans' Case Against Jesus

● The Romans may have been alarmed by Jesus' dramatic entry into Jerusalem when many people acclaimed him as leader and king. This could have been seen as a direct challenge to Roman rule.

● In front of Pilate, the Jews accused Jesus of causing trouble.
'We caught this man misleading our people, telling them not to pay taxes to the Emperor and claiming that he himself is the Messiah, a king. . . . With his teaching he is starting a riot among the people all through Judaea.'   Luke 23, 2,5

But all the gospels say that Pilate was not convinced by these arguments. So why did he agree that Jesus should be executed?

1 Pilate may have been afraid of an all-out riot if he went against the people's wishes. The crowd wanted Jesus to be killed.

2 Pilate had not found it easy to rule Judaea and he may have thought that if the Sanhedrin and the crowd got what they wanted they would be more willing to co-operate with him in the future.

3 Although Pilate agreed to Jesus' death, he literally washed his hands of the matter and refused to take responsibility for the decision. By doing this, he ensured that if there was any trouble, the Jews would get the blame.

THE CHRISTIAN
POINT OF VIEW

We have to take the Christian point of view into account because all our evidence about Jesus' trial and death comes from Christian sources, the gospels. We must remember that the gospel writers saw Jesus in a quite different light from the Jews and Romans. They, and Christians after them, believed that Jesus really was the Son of God and that he had come to earth to die and show God's love for the world. They also believed that Jesus rose from the dead after his execution.

How does this affect the evidence we have?

It explains some of the features of the gospel account which are difficult to understand. It explains

● Why Jesus told his disciples that he was going to die and why he appears to make no effort to avoid being arrested or to defend himself at his trial.

● Why he is shown as being innocent of any crime. From a Christian point of view there can be no question of Jesus being guilty of anything.

● Why the Jews are presented as being very quick to condemn Jesus.

● Why there is no explanation of the crowd's reasons for wanting Jesus to be executed.

● Why Pilate is shown as thinking Jesus was innocent. When the gospels were written, there was trouble between Christians, Jews and Romans. Perhaps the gospel writers did not want to offend the Romans by blaming them for Jesus' death.

How Jesus Died

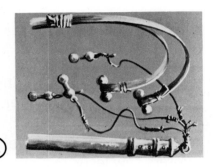

(A)

Jesus was condemned to death by crucifixion. This was a *very* painful way to die. Crucifixion was a Roman form of execution often used to punish rebellious slaves and common criminals. After he was condemned, Jesus was beaten by the Roman soldiers using whips like the ones in **A**.

(B)

Criminals were usually crucified at a place called Golgotha, which means 'the place of the skull' (**B**). Matthew, Mark and Luke say that the soldiers got a bystander, Simon of Cyrene (a place in North Africa), to carry the cross on which Jesus was to be crucified to Golgotha. John says Jesus carried his own cross. According to tradition, they walked along the street in Jerusalem which is called the Via Dolorosa or 'Street of Sorrows' today (**C**).

At Golgotha, Jesus was crucified. He was offered drugged wine to lessen the pain but he refused it.

(C)

In 1968, the bones of a man who had been crucified were discovered in a cemetery dating from the time of Jesus near Jerusalem. **D** shows one of the man's heel bones with a nail sticking out of it. These bones have helped experts understand how crucifixions were carried out. **E** is a picture of how it is thought this man was crucified.

(D)

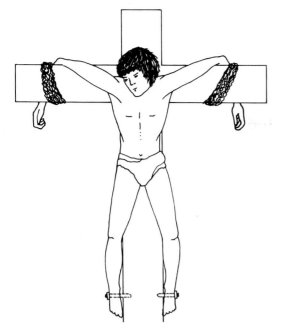

E

Crucifixion was a terrible way to die. The victim suffered great pain hanging on the cross. Sometimes he would hang there for days. Death, when it came, was usually by suffocation from liquids which built up in the lungs. To speed up the victim's death his legs would be broken.

Jesus seems to have died within about six hours of being nailed to the cross. During the time he hung there the gospels tell us he spoke seven times. **F** lists the things he said.

Because he died quickly, Jesus did not have his

legs broken, but, according to John's gospel, a soldier stuck a spear into his side to make sure he was dead before being taken off the cross. Blood and water came out of the wound which showed that he was dead.

❧ Things to do ❧

1 The gospels' accounts of the crucifixion of Jesus do not explain how he was fixed to the cross. But the evidence of John 20, 24–7 suggests that Jesus' crucifixion was different from that shown in **E**. What is the difference?

2 Imagine you are one of Jesus' followers watching him being beaten and being crucified. Write an account of what happened. Describe your feelings.

3 Imagine you are one of the soldiers who beats and crucifies Jesus. Describe what happened from this point of view. Remember you have probably crucified people before.

4 Study **F**. What was Jesus' mental state as he hung on the cross as shown by what he said?

F		
Forgive them, Father! They don't know what they are doing.	Said about the Jews and the Romans who had condemned him.	Luke 23, 34
I promise you that today you will be in Paradise with me.	Said to the thief who repented while being crucified next to Jesus.	Luke 23, 43
He is your son. . . . she is your mother.	Jesus entrusts his mother to the care of the disciple John.	John 19, 26–7
My God, my God, why did you abandon me?	Jesus calls out, quoting the words of Psalm 22.	Mark 14, 34 and Matthew 27, 46
I am thirsty.		John 19, 28
It is finished!		John 19, 30
Father! In your hands I place my spirit!		Luke 23, 46

The Turin Shroud

Could **A** be a picture of Jesus? It is the image on a long linen cloth called the Turin Shroud. Many people believe that this was the burial cloth, or *shroud*, Jesus was wrapped in after he died.

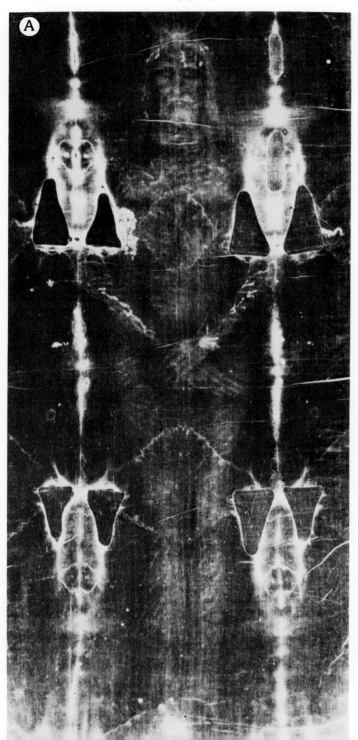

All over the world there are objects or *relics* which some people believe have a special connection with Jesus. Most of the relics are surrounded by a lot of legends and mysteries and it is impossible to tell which, if any, are genuine. More than one church has claimed to possess Jesus' shroud. What makes the one at Turin different?

Look at **A** again. This image is preserved in the cloth of the shroud and, so far, no one has been able to explain how it got there. The image was first noticed in 1898 when a young Italian photographer took a picture of the shroud and noticed the image appearing on the negative he developed. If you look very very closely at the shroud itself, you can see the faint image of a man. But the image is very much clearer in a photographic negative (**B** & **C**). Many people feel that the mysterious nature of the image is the sign of a miracle proving that this was the burial cloth of Jesus. Other people think the image is just a very clever forgery. Let us look at the evidence.

The image of the man has been closely studied. It has marks which suggest that the man had been crucified. There are also signs of beatings. The right eye was swollen and there were wounds on the face. There are marks of a lash and gashes that could have been caused by a 'crown of thorns'. The man's legs had not been broken and there is also a wound on the right side of the body. This matches some of the details in John's gospel. See **D**.

D *The soldiers went and broke the legs of the first man and then of the other man who had been crucified with Jesus. But when they*

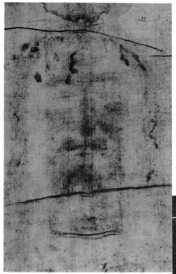

B Positive

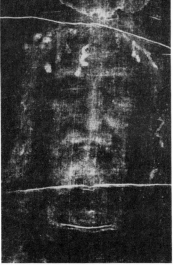

C Negative

In fact, there is no absolutely conclusive evidence about what the image is, how it was created and who it belonged to. There is one test which would help us know the date of the shroud. Scientists and archaeologists use a technique called carbon dating to help discover the age of something which was once living. The cloth was made from a plant called 'flax'. Carbon dating could be used to tell the date at which the flax was harvested. But carbon dating is not always entirely reliable and so far the church that owns the shroud has not allowed a test to be made.

Even if this test is done one day, it still would not tell us whether the image shows Jesus. It could not even prove that the image itself dates from Jesus' time. A medieval forger might have painted his picture on a very old cloth from the 1st century AD. We may never be able to prove whether the shroud shows Jesus, but it remains a fascinating mystery which many people believe is a sign of Jesus' special power.

came to Jesus, they saw that he was already dead so they did not break his legs. One of the soldiers, however, plunged his spear into Jesus' side, ...   John 19, 32–4

What evidence is there that the shroud is a forgery? Perhaps the shroud was made for one of the religious plays which were commonly held in the middle ages. These plays often included a re-enactment of Jesus' death and burial. Could the image be the faded remains of one of the painted cloths used in a play? Some traces of what could be paint have been found on the shroud but most scientists say that the image was not painted on to the cloth. Also, if it was a forgery it was a very clever one and no other medieval pictures of Jesus show such clever understanding of the human body. But this argument is not conclusive.

❧❧ Things to do ❧❧

1 Read the account of the crucifixion on the previous pages of this book. Also, if you can, look up the gospel accounts. Make a list of the details of Jesus' suffering. Match the features of the shroud to the list.

2 From what you have read, do you think the shroud is a forgery or the cloth Jesus was buried in? Give reasons for your answer.

3 If carbon dating tests showed that the shroud did not come from the time of Jesus, what effect, if any, do you think this would have on the Christian faith today?

Easter Day–What Happened?

(A) *In accordance with his own plan God had already decided that Jesus would be handed over to you. And you killed him by letting sinful men crucify him. But God raised him from death.*   Acts 2, 23–4

A is what the disciple Peter said to the Jews in Jerusalem at the start of the disciples' mission to convert people to Christianity.

Jesus' followers were convinced that Jesus was raised back to life three days after he was crucified. Christianity is based on this belief in Jesus' death and resurrection. What really happened after Jesus died on the cross?

As with almost all the evidence about Jesus, we must look at the gospel record. All four gospels describe how the tomb where Jesus' body was put was found empty. But each gospel gives a slightly different version of the event. Were the gospel writers relying on the memories of different people? **B** gives shortened versions of the gospel accounts.

The tomb may have been empty, but the disciples did not really believe that Jesus was alive again until he appeared and proved to their satisfaction that he was no ghost. **C** lists the appearances mentioned in the gospels.

(B)

Matthew
Mary Magdalen and the 'other Mary' go to the tomb on Sunday morning. When they get there, they see an angel roll away the stone which blocked the entrance. There were soldiers guarding the tomb to prevent the body of Jesus being stolen. They fall down in a faint. The angel tells them Jesus is raised from the dead. He shows them the empty tomb and sends them off to tell the other disciples.

Mark
Mary Magdalen, Mary the mother of James, and Salome go to the tomb on Sunday morning and find the stone rolled away from the entrance. Inside they find a young man in a white robe who tells them that Jesus has been raised from the dead. He tells them to tell the disciples that Jesus has gone to Galilee to await them there.

Luke
Mary Magdalen, Mary the mother of James, Joanna and other unnamed women go to the tomb early on Sunday. They find the stone rolled away. Then two men in shining clothes appear and tell them Jesus is raised back to life. When the women tell the disciples this no one believes them. But Peter goes to the tomb and finds it empty apart from the grave cloths.

John
Mary Magdalen goes to the tomb and finds the stone rolled away. She runs back to Peter and John and tells them Jesus' body has been taken away. Peter and John run to the tomb and find it empty apart from the grave cloths. They go home but Mary Magdalen stays outside the tomb. She looks in and sees two angels dressed in white who ask her why she is crying. She explains that Jesus' body has been taken away. At that moment she turns around and sees Jesus, but she does not recognise him until he says her name.

C The Resurrection Appearances

	Where	When	To whom
Matthew 28, 9–10	near the tomb, Jerusalem	Sunday morning	Mary Magdalen and 'the other Mary'
Matthew 28, 16–20	a hill in Galilee	no details	the remaining 11 disciples
Luke 24, 13–32	on road to Emmaus which was about 11km from Jerusalem	Sunday	2 disciples: Cleopas and another
Luke 24, 34	no details	Sunday	Simon
Luke 24, 36–53	Jerusalem	Sunday/ Monday	11 disciples and other followers
John 20, 11–18	near the tomb, Jerusalem	Sunday morning	Mary Magdalen
John 20, 19–25	Jerusalem indoors	Sunday evening	the disciples minus Thomas
John 20, 26–29	Jerusalem indoors	a week later	the disciples including Thomas
John 21, 1–22	on the shore of Lake Galilee	no details	Peter, John, James, Thomas, Nathanael and two others

Many people have doubted that the gospel records are really convincing evidence that Jesus rose from the dead. The accounts are not absolutely in agreement and Jesus only seems to have appeared to his followers. Can their evidence be trusted? What other explanations might there be for the empty tomb and the appearances of Jesus after his death? Here are some possible explanations.

1 *Jesus was not really dead when he was taken down from the cross.* This seems unlikely because the soldiers who crucified him would have known their jobs and the authorities would have wanted to make very sure that Jesus was dead. Could anyone have survived being speared in the side as John tells us Jesus was?

2 *Someone else was crucified in Jesus' place* (perhaps Simon of Cyrene who carried the cross). Again this is unlikely. There would have been many people who would have been able to recognise Jesus.

3 *The disciples stole the body and started the story of Jesus' resurrection to keep his message alive and embarrass the authorities.* According to Matthew, this rumour was spread by the chief priests and accepted by many Jews. But, as Matthew explains, this idea had already occured to the authorities and Pilate had posted guards at the tomb.

4 *The disciples went to the wrong tomb.* But they would have known where the leader they had followed for so long was buried.

5 *Someone else stole the body.* What could have been the motive?

continued on next page

D

None of these explanations are completely satisfactory. So did Jesus really rise from the dead? There is no precise proof of the resurrection because the exact details about what actually happened remain a mystery. But the disciples were convinced that Jesus had died and was raised back to life and was living amongst them again. Their lives were transformed. They believed that Jesus was still present in their lives as do all committed Christians today.

❧| Things to do |❧

1 a) Draw four columns, one for each gospel. Read **B** then list the details of each gospel story which agree with the details of at least one other gospel story.
b) What are the main differences between the four accounts in **B**? c) Which version of the discovery of the empty tomb do *you* think is most reliable? Why?

2 In Jesus' time, stories involving women were not taken very seriously. The gospel accounts all tell us that women found the empty tomb first. Does this make the account more or less reliable historically? Give reasons for your answer.

3 Do you think that any of the possible explanations on page 47 for the disappearance of Jesus' body are likely to be right? Could there be another explanation? Does it matter if there is no *historical* proof about what really happened on Easter day? Why?

4 Look at **D** which shows a tomb like the one in which Jesus was put. Imagine you are one of the first people to find Jesus' tomb empty. What would you say to the other disciples? How would you feel? What do you think might have happened? In class, act the scene where you tell the disciples that the tomb is empty.